Bigk - the Spider

Angela McAllister

Illustrated by Jess Mikhail

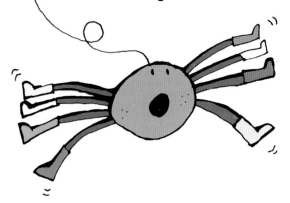

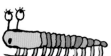

OXFORD
UNIVERSITY PRESS

1

Nothing scares me!

Spider played all day in the thorn
bush. He loved to swing on his
super-elastic thread.

'Look at me! I'm flying!'

All the bugs and beetles thought he
was a hero.

At home, Spider did kicks and spins.
'Watch this!' he cried.

'Very clever,' said Mum as she
untangled his legs. 'I wish you were
clever enough to find matching socks!'

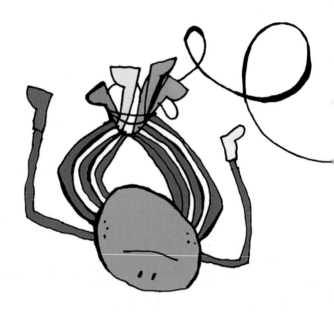

'Who cares about socks,' scoffed
Spider. 'I can jump from the treetops!'

'I want to jump from the treetops,
too!' said his little sister.

Spider laughed. 'Wait until you are
big and brave like me.'

'Show off,' said his sister. She didn't
like Spider's boasting, and she didn't
believe his stories.

One day, Spider noticed a house on the other side of the thorn bush.

'Stay away from there,' warned Dad. 'That's where the monsters live.'

'What sort of monsters?' asked Spider.

'Gigantic ones,' said Dad, 'with hundreds of fangs!'

Spider wanted to take another look.

'Don't go!' cried the bugs and beetles. 'The monsters will grab you! They'll stamp on you with their gigantic feet!'

'I'm not afraid,' said Spider. 'Nothing scares me.'

'Don't go!'

2
The monsters' house

Spider was excited. He wanted to
explore the monsters' house and have
a real adventure.

So he crept through the thorn bush
and tiptoed across the grass.

Suddenly a shadow fell over
Spider and he hid behind a leaf.

But it was only a sparrow.
Spider went on.
The monsters' house was very
quiet. Bravely, he stepped
inside...

The house was silent and still and Spider went exploring.

He peeped in every room, but he didn't see any monsters with fangs.

'Pah!' he said. 'This is boring.'

Spider sat down and scratched his leg.

All of a sudden the ground shook. **Thud! Thud! Thud!**

Spider trembled. 'Nothing scares m...me,' he gulped.

Then a gigantic monster appeared. It had fangs and stamping feet!

'Help!' cried Spider.

Help!

The monster lifted its foot and Spider shut his eyes.

'HELP!' screamed the monster.
'A SPIDER!' It shook with fear and its fangs rattled. Then it turned white and ran away.

Spider was amazed.

When Spider got home, he told his family about the monster.

'*I* scared it off!' he boasted. 'It looked at me and ran away.'

'I want to see the monster, too,' said his sister.

'No,' said Spider. 'You'd be too scared. You're even afraid of teeny-weeny bugs!'

3

Bigboots

Spider's story spread all over the thorn bush. Little bugs and beetles loved the tale of Spider and the monster. By morning, he was famous.

Now Spider wanted more adventures. He went back to the monsters' house and he hid in the plughole of the bath.

When another monster arrived, Spider jumped out.

This monster was all pink, but it screeched and ran away just like the first one.

Spider had fantastic fun. Scaring monsters was easy.

He climbed onto their pillows and tickled their ears.

He jumped into their breakfast.

He swung under their noses.

He popped out of their shoes.

Spider had a great time.

Spider's mum and dad were
not happy.

'You are always late for tea,'
grumbled Mum.

'You're getting too big for your
boots,' warned Dad.

'**Bigboots!**' cried Spider's sister. 'I don't believe you've ever seen a monster. You're just making it all up!'

Spider grinned. 'You just wish you were brave like me,' he said.

19

4
Look out!

One morning, Spider marched
into the monsters' house but no one
was there.

He sat in the bath. He had a doze in
a shoe. Then he hung in the doorway,
but there was nobody to scare.

Suddenly, Spider saw his sister creeping across the doorstep! She had followed him to the monsters' house. She *was* brave like him, after all.

Spider was just going to call out and tell her to be careful. Then he froze.

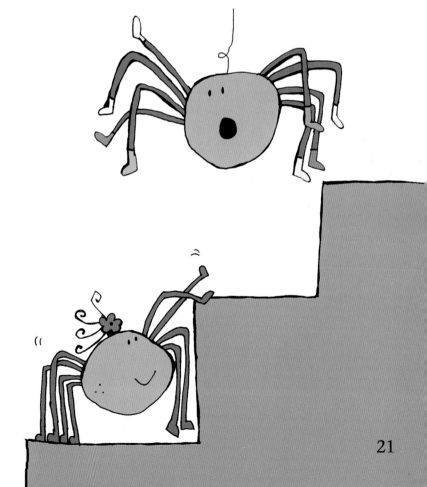

Out of the shadows crept a
teeny-weeny bug. Spider was
TERRIFIED of teeny-weeny bugs!
He shook like a jelly.

'Look out!' he said in a tiny voice,
but his sister didn't hear.

The teeny-weeny bug
crept up behind Spider's sister.
She took a step.
So did the teeny-weeny bug.
She took another step.
So did the teeny-weeny bug.
She turned around...

23

'Help!' screamed Spider's sister.

Suddenly, they heard,

'Thud! Thud! Thud!'

'The monsters are coming home,' cried Spider. 'Run!'

But his sister was so scared she couldn't move.

'I've got to save her,' thought Spider.

Then Spider remembered what his mother always said. 'Don't be afraid of teeny-weeny bugs. They are much smaller than you.'

Spider took a deep breath. He whizzed up to the top of the door.

'Watch out below!' he cried and he **swooped** down and grabbed hold of his sister.

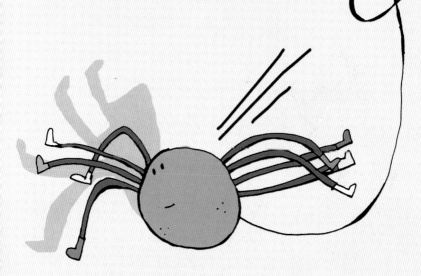

Spider grabbed hold of his sister, swung her out of the door and onto the grass.

'Thanks,' she said. 'I didn't believe you were brave, but you *really* are!'

'Well, *you* were brave to follow me,' said Spider, proudly.

5

Nothing scares us!

Spider and his sister went home. She told everyone how he had saved her.

'You're not even afraid of teeny-weeny bugs,' she said. 'Are you?'

'They're so *small*,' said Spider with a wink. 'I don't bother being scared of them!'

'Spider is a hero!' cried all the bugs and beetles.

'My sister's brave too,' said Spider. 'She went into the monsters' house alone.'

'Yes, nothing scares *us!*' said Spider's sister. She smiled at him happily.

Next morning, Spider's sister helped him find matching socks. Then he took her to the thorn bush to play.

'Take care,' said Mum. 'Don't swing too high.'

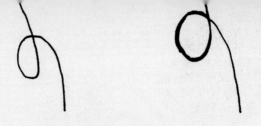

But they did! They swung
high, side by side. They were
brave and fearless together and
it was great!

When the teeny-weeny bug got
home, he told his family about
the spiders.

'I scared them off!' he boasted.
'Two of them!'

'I don't believe you,' said his sister.
'Next time, I'm coming with you!'

About the author

Lots of spiders live in my old house. I like them but my children are afraid, even though spiders are so small. I hope this story will help them to be braver. After all, it is the spiders' house too!